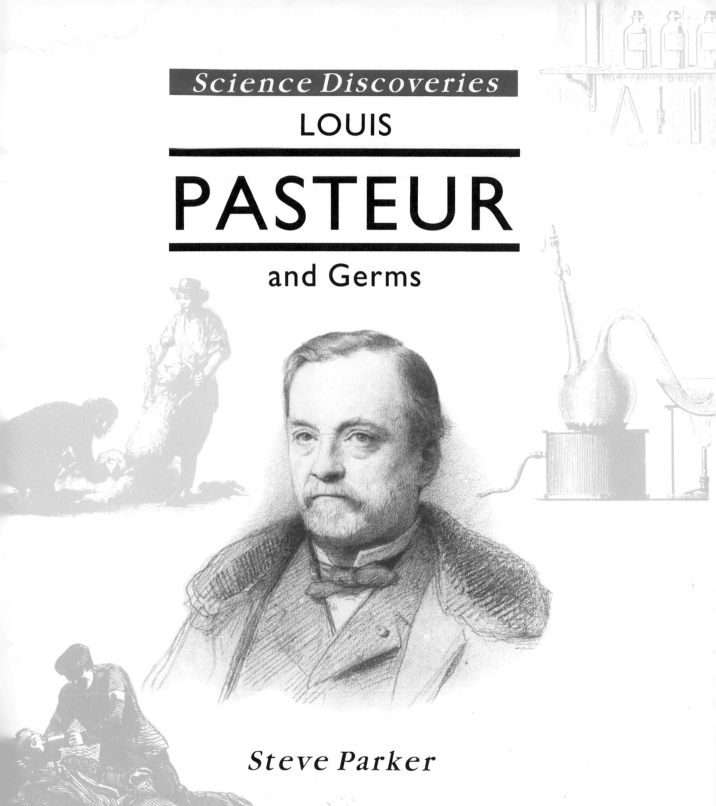

Science Discoveries

LOUIS

PASTEUR

and Germs

Steve Parker

🕮 Belitha Press

First published in Great Britain in 1993 by
Belitha Press Limited
31 Newington Green, London N16 9PU

Copyright © Belitha Press Limited 1993

Text © Steve Parker 1993

Illustrations/photographs copyright © in this
format by Belitha Press Limited 1993

ISBN 1 85561 170 8
Typeset by Chambers Wallace, London
Printed in China for Imago Publishing

British Library Cataloguing in Publication data
for this book is available from the British Library

Acknowledgements

Photographic credits:
Nick Birch 15 top left, 16 bottom
Bridgeman Art Library 19 bottom left Royal
    College of Surgeons, London
Mary Evans Picture Library 4 Town and Country
    Planning, 8 top and bottom, 10 bottom, 11 top,
    17 top, 19 centre, 22 top, 24 bottom
Giraudon, Paris 14 top Chateau Versailles,
    25 bottom Lauros-Giraudon/Chateau
    Versailles, 26 Musee D'Orsay, Paris
Robert Harding Picture Library 27 bottom
    Alfred Wolf
Hulton Deutsch Collection 1, 10 top
Hutchison Library 20 Anna Tully
Mansell Collection 17 bottom, 23 top
Musée Pasteur, Institut Pasteur, Paris 5 all, 24 top,
    25 top

Retrograph Archive, London 16 top Martin Breese
Ann Ronan Picture Library/Image Select
    11 bottom, 15 bottom, 18 bottom, 19 top,
    23 bottom
Royal College of Physicians 19 bottom right
Science Photo Library 11 centre Dr. Jeremy
    Burgess, 12 Jean-Loup Charmet, 15 top right,
    18 top Dr. Rosalind King, 22 bottom CNRI,
    27 top right NIBSC, 27 top left Sinclair
    Stammers

Cover montage supplied by Mary Evans Picture
Library, Mansell Collection, Ann Ronan Picture
Library/Image Select

Illustrations: Peter Bull 9, 14, 20;
Tony Smith 6-7, 13, 21
Editor: Rachel Cooke
Designer: Andrew Oliver
Picture researcher: Juliet Duff
Specialist adviser: Dr Perry Williams

Contents

La Rue des Arènes in Dole, a quiet town on the graceful River Doubs, east of Dijon, France. Louis' parents settled here in about 1815.

Introduction

"Michelle had a sore throat, probably a **virus**. She stayed at home so that we couldn't catch it."

"Keep the flies off your food; they carry **germs**."

"Blow your nose into a paper tissue. Remember: coughs and sneezes spread diseases!"

Today, we are used to the idea that germs cause illnesses. We know how to kill germs and stop diseases spreading. Yet this knowledge is less than 150 years old. Before then, people had quite different ideas about how diseases were caused. Scientists used **microscopes**, but they did not appreciate the nature of the germs and other tiny living things they saw through them.

Louis Pasteur was a French chemist who was to change this. He founded the science of microbiology – the study of living things such as **bacteria** and viruses, which can be seen only with the aid of a microscope. His work made possible many important advances in medicine, public health and hygiene. It has had immense effects on our daily lives, from the **vaccinations** that protect us against certain diseases, to the safe milk we pour on our breakfast cereal each morning.

Chapter One
The Early Years

Louis Pasteur was born on 27 December 1822, in Dole, eastern France. His father owned a tannery, making and preparing leather. He had been in the army and won medals, and he had a tremendous pride in France and the achievements of his nation. Louis shared his father's national pride and kept it throughout his life.

When Louis was still a child, the family moved to Arbois, where he attended the local primary and secondary schools. Family life was uneventful, and Louis was an average pupil. His early interest was art. He drew pictures in chalks and charcoal, and painted many portraits of his friends and family. At the age of 16 years, he was thinking about becoming a full-time artist. However, the principal at the college saw that Louis was a careful, willing student who thought clearly and logically. He advised the family that Louis should continue his education.

Louis was born in this humble house on the Rue des Tanneurs, Dole. In later life he attended a ceremony to unveil a plaque here, in his honour. The portraits of his parents (below) were painted by Louis himself.

The Pasteur house in Arbois, several kilometres south-east of Dole. Behind it were pits dug for the preparation of skins for tanning.

Colleges and Exams

In 1839, the young Pasteur went to the Royal College at Besançon. He passed his examinations to become a Bachelor of Arts, then Bachelor of Science. However, he was not very successful at the subject for which he would eventually become world-famous. His chemistry examination was marked "mediocre".

Louis intended to continue his studies in the scientific classrooms of the famous École Normale Supérieure in Paris. But in 1842, he was placed fifteenth out of the twenty-two new students the École accepted. He thought this was not good enough, so delayed his move to the École Normale Supérieure. Instead he became a part-time student and teacher at a Paris boarding school, and attended courses at the Lycée Saint Louis. Next year, 1843, he began his course at the École Normale Supérieure, ranked fourth in the class. It was an early sign of his competitive personality.

During his student years, Pasteur worked hard and sometimes topped his class, especially in physics, chemistry and mathematics. But he was not an outstanding student, merely "satisfactory". He gained his qualifications mainly by willpower and long hours of hard work. He became a Master of Science in 1845, and went on to an advanced degree in physical sciences. He obtained his Doctor of Science on 23 August 1847. He was making steady, if unspectacular, progress up the ladder of scientific qualifications.

Changing Plans

One of Pasteur's early influences was the well-known chemist Jean-Baptiste Dumas. Pasteur attended his lectures at the Sorbonne, along with 800 others – the lecture room was always full when Dumas spoke. Pasteur was impressed by Dumas' enthusiasm and careful preparation, his eloquence, and his way of making chemistry both exciting and mysterious. He remained a lifelong admirer of Dumas, and the two eventually became work colleagues and close friends.

Pasteur had always intended to teach and asked Dumas for a job as an assistant teacher. But soon his plans were changing. At the end of his time as a student at the École Normale Supérieure, his superiors said: "Will make an excellent professor [teacher]". But Louis' thoughts were turning away from teaching as a profession, toward experiments and laboratories, and the quest for new scientific knowledge.

A typical lecture scene during Pasteur's time as a student. He was so keen to enter the École Normale Supérieure that he arrived in Paris several days early, and slept in the empty students' dormitory.

Pasteur in 1865.

Chapter Two
A Brilliant Chemist

From about 1844-47, Louis Pasteur carried out his first important work in chemistry. He decided to investigate a puzzle involving tartrate **crystals**, obtained from **tartaric acid**, found in many fruits. German chemist Eilhard Mitscherlich had already shown that tartaric acid contained exactly the same chemical elements, in the same proportions, as another substance – **racemic (paratartaric) acid**. The puzzle was one difference between them. It involved a laboratory test using a special kind of light, called **polarized light**. When polarized light was shone through certain substances dissolved in water, it was rotated or "twisted". Tartaric acid rotated polarized light, but racemic acid did not. Why should this be?

The École Normale Supérieure in Paris, where Pasteur was student, and eventually administrator and director of scientific studies.

Mirror-Image Chemicals

Other chemists believed that crystals of tartaric acid and racemic acid were exactly the same shape. Pasteur guessed that he would find a tiny difference. He looked at them under the microscope. On close examination, racemic acid crystals were of two types. The slight difference between the types was in the arrangement of the flat faces, or **facets**. These were positioned exactly opposite to each other, like an object and its reflection in a mirror.

The crystals of tartaric acid, on the other hand, were all the same. In fact, they were identical to one of the racemic acid types.

Pasteur separated the two types of crystals by hand. One rotated polarized light to the left, and the other rotated it to the right. Racemic acid was a mixture of both types, so the lefts and rights cancelled each other out. This was the reason why racemic acid did not affect polarized light, but tartaric acid did.

Today, it may not seem an earth-shattering piece of research. But this type of work was a vital part of the chemical investigations of the time, and Pasteur had scored a first-time success. He was so delighted with his achievement, he rushed out of the laboratory and embraced the first person he met. On 22 May 1848, Pasteur presented his report on the work to the Paris Academy of Sciences.

The Beginnings of Stereochemistry

Pasteur's early work on crystals led chemists to realize that the properties of substances depend not only on the ingredients or chemical elements in them, but also on the way these elements are positioned in relation to each other. This was reflected in their crystal shape. It was the beginning of **stereochemistry**, that is, the study of the arrangement in space of the various different elements in a substance and how this affects the substance's chemical behaviour. This has become an important part of chemical analysis.

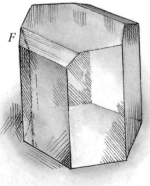

laevo-tartrate

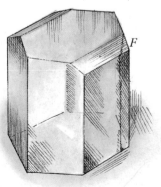

dextro-tartrate

Two types of crystals of the salt of racemic acid. As you can see in the diagram, the crystals are very similar to each other. The difference is that laevo*-tartrate with the facet F on its left is an exact mirror image of the* dextro*-tartrate where F is on the right. Pasteur was the first to spot this.*

Marie Laurent (Madame Pasteur) with her husband in 1889.

The Chemistry Institute at Strasbourg, where Pasteur arrived on 15 January 1850.

Family Life

In 1849, Pasteur became chemistry professor at a regional faculty (department) of the French university in Strasbourg. Here he met and, after a short court-ship, married Marie Laurent, the daughter of the rector at Strasbourg. They had five children: daughters Jeanne (1850), Cecile (1853), Marie-Louise (1858) and Camille (1863), and son Jean-Baptiste (1851). Only Jean-Baptiste and Marie-Louise survived to adulthood. Pasteur was deeply affected by the deaths of his young daughters, Jeanne in 1859 and Cecile in 1866, both from typhoid fever. This helped to spur him to his later research on human diseases.

Marie supported her husband in his work, taking notes and organizing his papers. He would complain that "the nights are too long", since the need for sleep kept him away from his beloved laboratory. Marie did not like Louis' long work hours. He once said to a colleague: "I am often scolded by Madame Pasteur [his wife], but I console her by telling her that I shall lead her to fame". Before he was 30 years old, Pasteur had developed an enormous faith that he would be a great scientist, like Galileo and Newton.

Wine is stored in barrels in order to mature. Wine making has long been a major French industry.

Researches in Fermentation

In 1854 Pasteur became dean and chemistry professor at the new Science Faculty in Lille. It was here, in the following year, that his keen interest in the chemistry of **fermentation** began. Amongst other things, fermentation describes the way sugary juices from grapes and other fruits bubble and turn into alcohol. The products, wines and beers, are part of French national tradition, and big money-earners.

It was French official policy to bring science to the service of industry and, in 1856, Pasteur received a query from Monsieur Bigo, head of one of the alcohol-making industries in Lille. His vats made alcohol from beet juice and other fruits and vegetables, but the products kept souring or spoiling (going bad). Could Pasteur, the well-known chemist, help?

At the time, most eminent scientists believed that fermentation was simply a **chemical reaction**. Tiny blobs had been seen in fermenting mixtures under the microscope, but these blobs – which are living things called yeasts – were thought to be unimportant; they were probably not even alive.

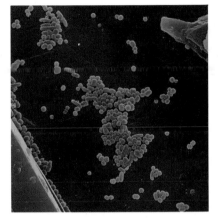

The rounded single cells of wine yeasts, responsible for fermenting wine, magnified about 1,000 times.

One of Pasteur's early designs for equipment to cool and ferment beer. The candle and spy-hole allow viewing of the contents.

Microbes

● **Microbes** and **micro-organisms** are living things that can be seen only with the aid of a microscope. Most microbes are less than one-tenth of a millimetre long, and most consist of only one **cell**.

● **Bacteria** are one main group of microbes, which Pasteur and his colleagues saw under the microscope. They live almost everywhere, in water and soil, and in other living things. Some bacteria are harmful, causing diseases. Others are helpful, for example, those that live in the gut and take part in the normal process of digestion.

● **Yeasts** are microbes which belong to the **fungus** group, which also includes mushrooms and toadstools. Much of Pasteur's work was on yeasts in wines and beers.

● **Germs** are now thought of as microbes that cause harm. So some bacteria are germs. The word germ was originally used to describe a seed of life, that is, life at its very beginning. The word in this sense is still used in the term "wheat germ".

Pasteur developed a theory that the tiny blobs were alive. They were yeast **microbes**, and as they lived, they turned sugar into alcohol. This was received with amusement, even horror, by some great scientists of the day. They made fun of Pasteur, asking whether his microbes were tiny animals that ate sugar, bubbled **carbon dioxide** gas out of their backsides, and expelled alcohol like we expel urine!

However, Pasteur went on to design careful experiments for testing his theory. He showed that fermentation did not happen unless the tiny blobs of living yeasts were present. If other microbes were present in the sugary juice, such as rod-shaped bacteria, then the fermentation was spoiled. The sugar turned not into alcohol, but **lactic acid**. This demonstrated that microbes could play a vital part in chemical changes. The science of microbiology was founded.

In 1856 Pasteur published his findings. The alcohol-making industries followed his advice about arranging conditions and preventing contamination of their vats. They were very grateful as their profits rose.

Pasteur "discovers the law of fermentation". He showed that microbes are responsible for spoiling the wine.

Edité par la CHOCOLATERIE D'AIGUEBELLE (Monastère de la Trappe-Drôme)

PASTEUR DÉCOUVRE LA LOI DES FERMENTS

Chapter Three
The Discovery of Germs

In *Mémoire sur la fementation appelée lactique* (Report on lactic fermentation) published in 1858, based on his work in Lille, Pasteur suggested that different microbes caused different types of fermentation – and that microbes might also cause various diseases. This was a foundation for the **germ theory of disease**, developed over many years.

By this time, Pasteur had returned to Paris. He became administrator and director of scientific studies at his old college, the École Normale Supérieure. He continued the study of yeasts and fermentation. His laboratory was a small attic room, and his incubator for growing microbes in warmth was an under-stair cupboard! But his skills at practical work overcame these limitations.

Pasteur was now a very ambitious man, confident, and ready to take on challenges and argue in public with his competitors. Colleagues spoke of his strong personality and enthusiasm, which inspired his friends, but which also made enemies.

Pasteur's attic laboratory at the École Normale Supérieure, in about 1858.

Napoleon III, French Emperor from 1852 to 1870.

Killing Germs With Heat

During the mid-1860s, Pasteur made one of his greatest discoveries. In 1863 he was asked by Napoleon III, the ruler of France's Second Empire, to help the French wine-makers. They were losing vast amounts of money because after fermentation, the wines kept turning sour. He discovered that contaminating microbes in the wine caused this souring – and that they could be destroyed by heat. The idea was extended to other perishable foods and drinks. These could be preserved by careful heating, to kill any harmful microbes they contained.

Pasteur developed the process now named after him, **pasteurization** (see panel). The wine-makers were suspicious of the "small bearded professor with the microscope", but they soon took up the process when its success was revealed.

Pasteurization

This process uses heat to kill off microbes in foods and drink, which would otherwise multiply and spoil them. Carried out correctly, it should have little effect on appearance or taste.

In the 1860s, Pasteur showed that heating wine or beer above 57°C (135°F) would kill any germs in it. This meant the wine and beer would keep much longer without going bad.

Today, milk, and many milk and egg products, are pasteurized. A modern HTST (high temperature, short time) pasteurizing machine heats milk to 72°C for 15 seconds, then cools it to below 10°C.

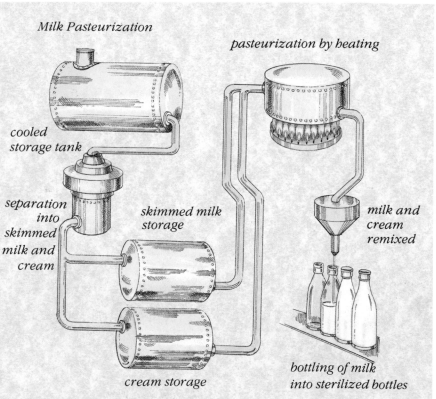

Milk Pasteurization

pasteurization by heating

cooled storage tank

separation into skimmed milk and cream

skimmed milk storage

milk and cream remixed

cream storage

bottling of milk into sterilized bottles

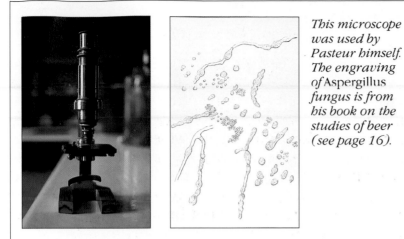

This microscope was used by Pasteur himself. The engraving of Aspergillus fungus is from his book on the studies of beer (see page 16).

Life From Nothing?

At this time, Pasteur became concerned with the notion of **spontaneous generation** (see panel), simply, that life could appear from non-living matter. His experiments showed that "clean air" contained floating microbes, **spores** and other living things. These could be trapped in **asbestos** filters, and grown on special **nutrient** substances called **culture media**, in laboratory equipment.

Pasteur also tested nutrient liquids, which would normally go bad through bacterial action. He showed they remained unchanged, even for months, if they were first sterilized by heat, and then kept in glass vessels with "swan necks" or special seals. The swan necks allowed in the oxygen necessary for life, but kept out microbe-bearing dust particles. No life appeared.

On 7 April 1864, at the Sorbonne, Pasteur used the results of his experiments to argue against spontaneous generation. Referring to the still-clear liquid, in which life had not spontaneously appeared, Pasteur said: "I have kept from it the only thing man cannot produce . . . the germs which float in the air."

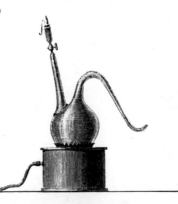

A swan-necked flask like that Pasteur used in his studies of spontaneous generation.

Spontaneous Generation

The idea of spontaneous generation said that under certain conditions, life could appear from simple non-living ingredients. It had developed in ancient times, to describe how maggots appeared in meat, and meal-worms in grain stores.

Gradually, experiments showed that creatures such as maggots hatched from tiny eggs laid by flies. By Pasteur's time no one believed in spontaneous generation of this kind. But some believed that microbes appeared spontaneously in nutrient-rich broth. Pasteur helped to show that the microbes floated onto the broth, unseen in the air.

Today, many scientists accept a modified version of the theory of spontaneous generation. Modern views on **evolution** imply that the first simple life-forms appeared from non-living substances, at a very early stage in the Earth's history. This explains the origin of life itself.

Rewards – and Disaster

In 1867 Napoleon III created a laboratory of physical chemistry for Pasteur at the École Normale Supérieure. It was a great honour for the chemist, who always had tremendous national pride. At this time, he took up the post of chemistry professor at the Sorbonne, the University of Paris, but continued to work in his new laboratory at the École Normale.

Then at the age of 45, on 19 October 1868, he suffered a stroke. This gradually paralyzed the left side of his body. However, he still continued his work.

The huge wine vats and bottling equipment at a French vineyard, in about 1880. Pasteur's research helped reduce wastage in wine production.

Modern pasteurization vessels process hundreds of litres of milk or other liquids every second.

Bouchage et dégorgeage.
Véritable Extrait de Viande Liebig.

Helping French Industries

In 1876 Pasteur published *Études sur la bière, ses maladies, et causes qui les provoquent* ("Studies on beer, its diseases, and the causes that provoke them"). This described how some microbes, unlike the vast majority of living things, did not need **oxygen** to live. Indeed, they perished if oxygen was present. Pasteur had discovered what we now call **anaerobic microbes**, which cause living matter to rot.

His work on fermentation and preservation had enormous benefits to the French food and drink industries. Through improvements in beer and wine production, vast amounts of money were saved.

Chapter Four
Preventing Disease

During his research into fermentation, Louis Pasteur was also active in other areas of science. Foremost was his study of disease, first in animals, then in humans.

The Curse of Anthrax

Anthrax is a serious illness caused by the germ *Bacillus anthracis*. In Pasteur's day it affected many cattle, sheep, horses, goats and similar animals, often causing death. People who worked closely with these animals, or handled their products, such as skins and wool, were also at risk from it. They suffered sore, swollen areas on the body, fever, in some cases pneumonia, blood poisoning, and the risk of death.

In 1876 the German scientist Robert Koch discovered that the germs responsible for anthrax could be grown in the laboratory. Koch was a general physician in Prussia, who built upon much of Pasteur's work on germ theory. Koch showed that certain bacteria were responsible for particular diseases, and he identified, named and grouped them.

Saving Silk

Silk is made from the fine fibres in the cocoons spun by silkworms (not worms, but the caterpillars of the silkmoth). In the 1860s, a disease of silkworms called **pebrine** reduced the output of France's valuable silk industry by six-sevenths. From 1865, Pasteur spent several years in the south of France. He looked for the germs responsible for pebrine, and devised ways of keeping the silkworm cages free of the disease.

Robert Koch at work. He received a Nobel prize for his work on bacteria in 1905.

17

The rod-shaped Bacillus anthracis *bacteria responsible for anthrax, magnified about 500 times. They have been stained with a laboratory dye to make them easier to see.*

In the meantime, Pasteur suggested that the spread of anthrax could be reduced by burning the bodies of its animal victims, rather than burying them or leaving them to rot. His experiments showed that resistant spores of the anthrax bacteria stayed in the soil, spread by earthworms and windblown dust, for many years.

The Road to Vaccination

In 1880, summer holidays delayed one of Pasteur's experiments on a disease known as **fowl cholera**, which affected chickens. His assistant Charles Chamberland forgot to inject some chickens with germs, and did so when he returned after the break. Strangely, the birds did not die. They became ill, but then recovered.

Pasteur devised a theory. The cholera-causing germs had been weakened, or attenuated, probably by exposure to air through the summer holidays. Then thinking of the work of Edward Jenner (see panel) he injected the same hens with fresh cholera germs. They survived. Another group of birds, new from the market, died when injected with the fresh cholera germs. Somehow the earlier dose of weakened germs made the first batch of chickens resistant to the disease.

This work was immensely significant. It paved the way for the process of vaccination and **immunization**.

Following the work of Pasteur and his colleagues, vaccination soon became established and even fashionable. This illustration shows free vaccination against smallpox using the fluid from cowpox sores, on the premises of a French magazine in 1905.

Sheep being vaccinated against anthrax, in about 1882. Pasteur's work helped to save the lives of thousands of farm animals.

In 1881, Pasteur and his co-workers developed further methods for weakening germs, in this case, the bacteria of anthrax. In a famous experiment in May, a group of 25 sheep were given the weakened anthrax germs; another group of 25, kept in the same conditions, were not. Later, all the sheep were given the full-strength anthrax bacteria. All those which had received the weakened bacteria survived. Nearly all the others died from anthrax. This was the first use of artificially-weakened germs, in a vaccine, to give protection against the same disease later. Pasteur and his team had no idea how the protection, which we now call immunity, developed. But they reasoned that it could save human lives.

Initially, fun was made of Jenner's ideas. People claimed that those receiving his vaccine would become part-cow!

In Honour of Jenner

In about 1796, English physician Edward Jenner had developed a method of protecting people against smallpox. He gave them a weaker form of the illness, called cowpox or *vaccinia*, which usually affected cattle and people who worked with them. After developing mild cowpox, these people were resistant to the much more serious smallpox.

Pasteur suggested that the term vaccination should be extended to cover any process using weakened germs to make the body resistant – immune – to the full-strength ones.

The hand with cowpox sores from which Jenner made his first smallpox vaccine.

Edward Jenner (1749-1823)

The process of immunization

The germs that cause a disease are isolated.

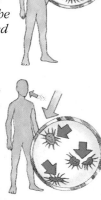

The germs are weakened or disabled.

In the vaccination, the weakened germs are injected into the body.

The body's immune-defence processes destroy the weakened germs.

The body can now destroy even the full-strength germs.

People queue for vaccinations in Nigeria. Large-scale vaccination offers the best hope of conquering many major infectious diseases.

Vaccination and Immunity

The work of Edward Jenner and Louis Pasteur has led directly to the life-saving immunizations of today. In the process of vaccination, you are given an injection or preparation of specially weakened or disabled germs. You only suffer very slightly, if at all, from the disease. But your body reacts as though the germs are normal, full-strength ones. It develops ways of killing these particular germs quickly. Next time they appear, even if they are full strength, they are soon inactivated. You are unlikely to catch the disease. This is called immunity.

Today, we are usually vaccinated during childhood against diseases such as diphtheria, tetanus, pertussis (whooping cough), polio, measles, mumps and rubella (german measles), and possibly tuberculosis.

Chapter Five
Reducing Human Suffering

Medicine in Pasteur's time had its dangers. Some treatments were more likely to kill patients than cure them. However, through the nineteenth century, doctors and scientists made steady progress in reducing the risks.

In 1847, Hungarian doctor Ignaz Semmelweiss reduced the spread of childbed (puerperal) fever, which affected many women with new babies. He suggested that before attending a new birth, the doctor should wash his hands! It may seem obvious today, because now it is always done; but at the time, doctors did not understand about germs and infection.

By 1865, British surgeon Joseph Lister was the first to use **carbolic acid (phenol)** on wounds during surgery. The carbolic acid acted as an **antiseptic**, or germ-killer. It prevented the wounds becoming infected by germs from the air, or on the hands and instruments of the surgeons. This quickly reduced the death rate after operations. Lister derived his ideas on antiseptics partly from Pasteur's work on microbes in the air.

In 1871, France lost the Franco-Prussian war. (Prussia is now part of Germany.) The French surgeons in the army hospitals were urged to adopt the practices of Lister by sterilizing their instruments and their patients' wounds. Despite this, only 3,000 patients survived of the 13,000 who had surgery! Over the next fifty years this type of statistic was to improve dramatically.

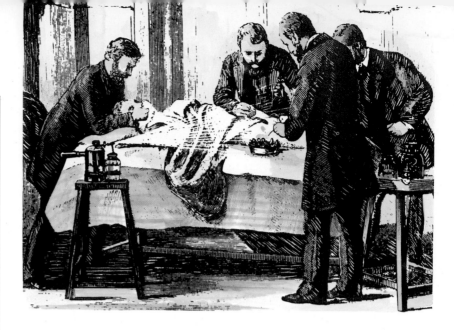

Surgeons use the "Lister spray" of carbolic acid (phenol), in about 1882.

The Mystery Germs

The germ theory was so successful that it was used to explain diseases like measles and rabies, that spread as though they were caused by microbes – but no one could find them. It was suggested that the microbes were too small to be seen under the microscopes of the time, and too small even to be trapped by special chemical filters. These theoretical microbes were called "filterable viruses". For many years after Pasteur, they were studied by their effects on laboratory chemicals and living things. Not until the invention of the more powerful **electron microscopes**, in this century, could people see viruses directly.

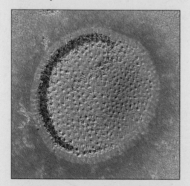

An artificially-coloured electron microscope view of a single virus. This is the type of virus that causes influenza ('flu), magnified 200,000 times.

The Germ Theory of Disease

Pasteur made sense of these medical advances, and encouraged a fuller understanding of illness, through the germ theory of disease. In 1878 he published *La théorie des germes et ses applications à la médicine et la chirurgie* ("The germ theory and its application to medicine and surgery").

The germ theory states that certain diseases are caused by germs. These get into, or infect, the body. If not neutralized by the body's defence system, they multiply and cause illness. Each disease is caused by a different type of germ. In Pasteur's time, these proposals were a tremendous breakthrough in the understanding of illness.

The theory was first applied to bacteria but it was soon being extended to cover other types of microbes, such as **protozoa** and also fungi.

In 1882, Robert Koch found the cause of the widespread and deadly tuberculosis (TB). It was a bacterial germ, duly named *Mycobacterium tuberculosis*. This was the first definite link between a germ and a human disease. Soon the laboratories of Pasteur, Koch and others developed vaccines against diseases such as cholera, tuberculosis, tetanus and diphtheria.

Research into Rabies

In 1882 Pasteur and his assistants tried to find the microbe which they assumed was the cause of rabies. They thought it was present in the saliva (spit) of infected dogs, and that it was spread by bites. But they could not see the germ under the microscope.

Their research showed that the rabies "agent" was also present in dogs' brains and nerves. They discovered that, like other germs, it could be weakened – in this case, by drying the nerve tissue. This suggested a way of producing an anti-rabies vaccine.

On 6 July 1885, after successful experiments with the anti-rabies vaccine in dogs, Pasteur tried it on a human. A young boy, Joseph Meister, had been bitten 14 times by a rabid dog. His mother pleaded with Pasteur to save him. It was a terrible decision. Had the boy caught rabies from the bites? If not, might the vaccine actually *give* him rabies? Pasteur decided to proceed.

Sixty hours after the bites, Joseph received the first of 12 anti-rabies injections. The vaccines were made from the spinal nerves of rabbits. The boy survived. A vaccine of the type developed by Pasteur is still used today. It is given to people who may have been infected, but only before they show signs of the disease. Once someone becomes ill with rabies, showing the virus has gained hold, death is the usual outcome.

The "Mad Dog" Disease

Rabies is dangerous and frightening. It affects animals such as dogs, cats, foxes, skunks and racoons, as well as people. People may catch the virus after being bitten by an infected animal. The disease affects the brain and nerves. About 10-50 days after being infected, the person becomes depressed and restless, then very excitable with fever, muscle spasms, convulsions, extra salivation and paralysis. He or she becomes very thirsty but cannot drink, because of the throat spasms. This led to another name for the illness, hydrophobia, meaing "fear of water".

The picture above shows one of the dogs to which Pasteur gave his anti-rabies vaccine.

Pasteur watches as an assistant vaccinates Joseph Meister.

Chapter Six

The Later Years

Pasteur and his family in the garden at Arbois, 1892

Throughout his career, Pasteur was never one to shy away from arguments. These were not always simply scientific disagreements. Pasteur's great patriotism made disputes with Robert Koch over anthrax vaccination bitterly personal. Koch had been a member of the Prussian armed forces that defeated the French in 1871.

Similarly, in later years, Pasteur fell out with a close colleague, Emile Roux. Roux had greatly helped Pasteur in his work on rabies and cholera but a personal wrangle developed over Roux's claims that Pasteur had stolen his ideas and equipment designs.

True to his belief in the greatness of France, Pasteur's scientific achievements brought many benefits to his nation. The chemist-turned-microbiologist was now a world figure. He travelled to the Congress of Hygiene in 1882 in Geneva, to report on ways of weakening viruses. Two years later, despite his continuing paralysis, he spoke before the International Congress of Medicine in Copenhagen, on vaccines for harmful microbes.

Controversies over Rabies

In 1888 Pasteur became the first director of the new *Institut Pasteur,* the Pasteur Institute, in Paris. It had been funded by international donations and by government grants, in gratitude for his work, but not without problems. Pasteur's view of rabies and its vaccine had been challenged by scientists, governments and the public alike. How did he know the vaccinated people were infected with rabies in the first place? The suspected rabies germs were too small to be detected, and many people bitten by mad dogs never developed rabies.

There was also opposition from people who were against experiments on animals, because of the way the rabies virus was grown in live rabbits.

During 1888, Pasteur would spend his afternoons watching the building of the Pasteur Institute.

Final Honours

Pasteur's work to support his views was exhausting, and took its toll on him. The year of 1892 was celebrated by a "Pasteur Jubilee" at the Sorbonne in Paris, on his 70th birthday. His memory and health were now failing, after a second attack of paralysis in 1887. During the summer of 1894 he visited the family home at Arbois for the final time. He was still director of the Pasteur Institute when he died on 28 September 1895. He was greatly honoured at his funeral, and buried in a tomb within the building.

The funeral of Louis Pasteur held in great state at the Palace of Versailles.

Chapter Seven
Pasteur in Perspective

The momentous achievements for which Louis Pasteur is remembered are not confined to one scientific area. He was a founder of stereochemistry, with his work on tartaric acid, and of microbiology. His proposal that diseases are caused by germs was one of the most important in the history of medicine, and it is a foundation of modern medical thinking. When a new illness is discovered that seems to be transferred from person to person, such as Legionnaire's disease or AIDS, researchers at once look for the causative germs.

Pasteur was a tireless experimenter. He spent many long hours in the laboratory carrying out chemical processes, looking down the microscope, and making notes. He had great powers of concentration.

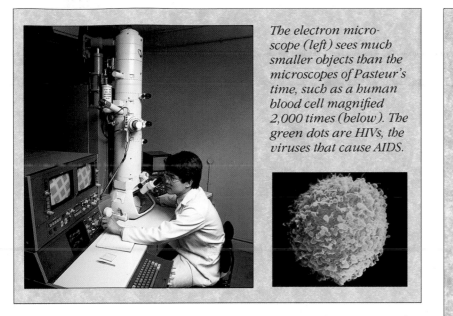

The electron microscope (left) sees much smaller objects than the microscopes of Pasteur's time, such as a human blood cell magnified 2,000 times (below). The green dots are HIVs, the viruses that cause AIDS.

Preserving Food and Drink

Pasteur's work on fermentation advanced the understanding of how beer, wine, bread and other foodstuffs are made. He showed how procedures could be devised to keep foods and drinks from spoiling or going bad. This has saved vast amounts of money for the food and drink industries, and innumerable cases of illness for consumers.

Building on the work of Jenner, Pasteur and his colleagues made possible the process of vaccination, which has doubtless saved millions of lives through the years. Over the last century, diseases such as cholera, tuberculosis and rubella, have become easy to prevent, whilst smallpox has been eradicated.

In 1967 the World Health Organization began a campaign of mass vaccination and treatment against smallpox. The numbers of sufferers gradually went down. At last, in 1979, the world was declared "smallpox-free". There are still some smallpox viruses – but they are locked in research laboratories. Through the work of Pasteur and others, many more diseases may be similarly controlled.

A World Centre for Science

At first, the main work of the Pasteur Institute was research and treatment of rabies, following methods established by Pasteur himself. The Institute soon became a world centre, not only for research into the prevention and treatment of diseases, but also for the production of vaccines, and for work in general microbiology. It is still based in Paris, and it is closely associated with the Pasteur Hospital there. The Institute and Hospital are fitting tributes for a man who made enormous advances in many areas of science, and who did so much to ease the burden of human suffering.

A scientist wearing protective mask and gloves, at work at the Pasteur Institute, Paris.

The World in Pasteur's Time

	1800-1825	**1826-1850**
Science	**1804** Richard Trevithick builds an early type of steam locomotive **1821** Michael Faraday demonstrates the principle of the electric motor **1822** Louis Pasteur is born	**1826** Joseph Niépce takes the first photograph, on a metal plate **1831** Charles Darwin sets sail on his round-the-world voyage in the *Beagle*
Exploration	**1803** The first European settlers arrive in Tasmania **1818** John Ross and other expeditions fail to find the North-West Passage, following a reward of £20,000 offered by George III of England	**1831** James Ross discovers the magnetic North Pole **1837** Beer and Madler make the first accurate map of the Moon **1847** The first reports of gorillas reach Europe from Africa
Politics	**1815** Napoleon's French army is defeated by Wellington at the Battle of Waterloo **1821** Mexico and Peru declare independence from Spain	**1833** British parliament abolishes slavery **1848** The July revolution topples Louis Philippe, France's last king, and establishes the Second Republic
Art	**1814** Franz Schubert completes his first opera at the age of 17 **1816** Jane Austen writes *Emma* **1820** *Venus de Milo* statue, over 2,000 years old, is discovered on the Greek island of Melos	**1843** The tuba becomes a regular member of the orchestra **1844-5** Alexandre Dumas finishes *The Three Musketeers* and *The Count of Monte Cristo*

1851-1875	1876-1900
1861 The first daily weather forecasts are issued, in Britain	**1877** Thomas Edison invents first versions of the gramophone
1862 Richard Gatling patents his machine gun	**1880** The protozoa that cause malaria are found to be carried by certain kinds of mosquito
1869 Dmitri Mendeleev publishes the first version of the periodic table of chemical elements	**1895** Louis Pasteur dies
1853 David Livingstone discovers the Victoria Falls of the Zambezi river	**1877** Astronomers see and map the "canals" of Mars
1869 American Union Pacific Railway crosses the continent	**1884** Greenwich Mean Time becomes the basis of the world time zones
	1883 The island of Krakatoa, South-East Asia, disappears in a huge volcanic eruption
1857 The Indian Mutiny fails to throw off British rule	**1876** General Custer makes his last stand against the Sioux at the Battle of Little Bighorn
1864 Jean Dunant founds the International Red Cross in Switzerland	**1879** Europeans finally defeat the Zulus in South Africa
1871 France is defeated in the Franco-Prussian War	
1853 Richard Wagner begins to compose *The Ring of the Nibelung,* a cycle of four operas, that takes him over 20 years	**1886** Auguste Rodin finishes his sculpture *The Kiss*
1872 Claude Monet paints *Impression: Sunrise,* and the type of painting known as Impressionism is named from it	**1888** Vincent Van Gogh paints his famous series of sunflower paintings
	1890 Henrik Ibsen's play *Hedda Gabler* is first performed

29

Glossary

anaerobic microbes: microscopic living things that do not need *oxygen* to survive and even die in its presence, unlike all other living things.

anthrax: a disease that affects mainly farm animals and sometimes people, caused by *bacteria*. Among its effects are sore, raw areas of skin, and severe chest problems.

antiseptic: a chemical used to kill or disable germs.

asbestos: a type of mineral fibre, usually containing chemicals known as silicates. It has uses in laboratory and chemical processes, insulation and fire-proofing.

bacteria (singular **bacterium**): a group of *microbes* which live almost everywhere. There are many thousands of different kinds. Some are harmful and cause diseases.

carbolic acid (phenol): a chemical with the formula C_6H_5OH, which is usually in the form of white *crystals* that can dissolve in water. Carbolic acid was one of the first *antiseptics* and is still used as a germ-killer.

carbon dioxide: one of the gases in the air. It is colourless with hardly any smell. It is given out by living things, from *yeasts* to humans, and when anything containing carbon burns.

cell: the smallest unit of life, or part of a living thing, only visible under a *microscope*. Some living things are just one cell, like *bacteria* and *yeasts*. The human body is made of millions upon millions of different cells.

chemical reaction: when two or more substances combine or interact together in some way, to form different products. An example is coal (carbon, C) reacting with *oxygen* (O_2) to form *carbon dioxide* (CO_2), in the chemical reaction we call burning.

crystal: a solid substance with a regular shape or form, with flat sides and sharp edges and corners. Different substances have crystals of different shapes and colours.

culture media: substances for growing *microbes*, usually watery or jelly-like, used in laboratories and factories. They contain all the *nutrients* that the microbes need to multiply.

electron microscope: a very powerful *microscope* that uses beams of particles called electrons rather than light. It can see in more detail than a light microscope.

evolution: changes with time, especially in animals, plants and other living things.

facets: the faces or flat surfaces on a crystal.

fermentation: the breaking down of certain substances into others caused by the action of microbes. Amongst other things, we use fermentation to make wines, beers and breads.

fowl cholera: a severe digestive infection caused by a *bacteria*, that affects fowl (chickens and similar birds).

fungus (plural **fungi**): a member of one of the main groups, or kingdoms, of living things. In the past, fungi have been grouped with plants but nowadays they are usually put in a group of their own. Unlike plants, they feed by breaking down or rotting other living things. Mushrooms, toadstools, mildews, rusts and yeasts are all fungi.

germ: any microbe that causes disease.

germ theory of disease: the proposal that, for the group of diseases called infections, each type of disease is caused by a certain type of germ. For example, tuberculosis is caused by the tuberculosis bacterium *Mycobacterium tuberculosis*.

immunization: the process of becoming immune, or resistant, to a disease – see *vaccination*. When immune, the body has the ability to kill quickly the microbes that cause the disease.

lactic acid: a substance with the chemical formula $C_3H_6O_3$, also known as 2-hydroxypropanic acid. It is made by the *fermentation* processes of some *bacteria* and also in muscles when they are very active.

microbe or **micro-organism:** a living thing that is so small it can only be seen under the microscope.

microscope: a device that magnifies very small things, making them look hundreds or thousands of times bigger than they really are.

molecule: the smallest particle of a substance that can exist by itself and still have all the chemical properties of that substance.

nutrient: "food", the substances a living thing needs to survive and grow.

organic chemistry: the study of compounds that contain carbon. Carbon compounds are found in all living *cells*.

oxygen: a colourless gas with no smell that makes up about one-fifth of the air around us. The vast majority of living things need oxygen in order to survive.

pasteurization: treating milk and similar substances with heat, to destroy harmful microbes.

pebrine: a disease of silkworms, the caterpillars of the silk moth, caused by the *protozoa* named *Nosema bombycis*. Tiny dark spots grow on and in the caterpillars' bodies, and they usually die before spinning their silken cocoons.

physiology: the scientific study of the processes of life in animals and plants.

polarized light: light in which the up-and-down motions of the light waves are all parallel or travelling in the same direction. Light waves usually form a random pattern.

protozoa: a group of *microbes*. They are single-celled animals.

racemic (paratartaric) acid: a mixture of the two forms of *tartaric acid*.

spontaneous generation: when living things appear to develop from non-living substances.

spores: microscopic structures produced by certain living things, such as bacteria and fungi. Under the right conditions, they grow into new versions of their "parent".

stereochemistry: the study of the arrangement of the different elements in a substance and how this affects the substance's chemical behaviour.

tartaric acid: a crystal substance with the chemical formula $C_4H_6O_6$. It is formed in grapes and other fruits. It occurs in two forms. The *dextro*-tartaric acid bends *polarized light* to the right; the mirror-image crystal *laevo*-tartaric acid bends it to the left.

vaccination: the technique of giving a person (or other living thing) weakened forms of a germ, such as a bacteria, to bring about *immunization*.

virus: minute things that cause some diseases. They are smaller than *bacteria* and other *microbes*, and can only be seen with an *electron microscope*. All viruses are harmful, because they can only multiply by taking over and destroying the cells of living things.

yeasts: microscopic blob-like *fungi*, each consisting of a single *cell*. Some types of yeasts are useful, being involved in *fermentation*.

Index